You Can Do It!

A Book to Help You Do Just About Anything

★ American Girl™

Published by Pleasant Company Publications

Copyright © 2006 by American Girl, LLC

Questions or comments? Call 1-800-845-0005,
visit our Web site at **americangirl.com**,
or write to Customer Service, American Girl, 8400 Fairway Place,
Middleton, WI 53562-0497.

Printed in China

06 07 08 09 10 11 LEO 10 9 8 7 6 5 4 3 2 1

Editorial Development: Erin Falligant, Michelle Watkins

Art Direction & Design: Chris Lorette David

Production: Mindy Rappe, Kendra Schluter, Jeannette Bailey,
Judith Lary

Illustrations: Tracey Wood

Special thanks to consultant
Patti Kelley Criswell, M.S.W.

Dear American girl,

Do you want to get better grades or run faster
on the soccer field? Grow your nails or find
a new hairstyle? Make a new friend or be
a *better* friend to your best friend?

Whether your goals are big or small, you CAN make them happen.

This book will show you how. You'll discover how to choose
goals that are right for you, right now, and how to go after
them one step at a time. You'll learn tricks for facing challenges
head-on, asking for help when you need it, and
staying motivated from start to finish.

Ready to get started? We'll be right there
beside you, cheering you on!

Your friends at American Girl

When you
see this pencil,
it's time to do some
writing in your
You Can Do It!
Journal.

Pay attention to your dreams.

What do you think about when you're spending time alone? What do you daydream about on your way to school in the morning or before you fall asleep at night?

Pay attention to your dreams, because **they tell you what makes you happy.** They show you what you would do or become if nothing stood in your way.

Start a **dream list** of all the things you want to do or be, no matter how big or faraway they may seem.

Pull out your journal, find a quiet place, and finish the sentences on pages 2 through 5.

To make a

dream

come true,
turn it into a

goal.

START STRONG

What's a dream?

A dream is what you would like to have happen someday.

What's a goal?

A goal is what you decide to make happen this week, this month, or this year (sometime soon).

You might dream of 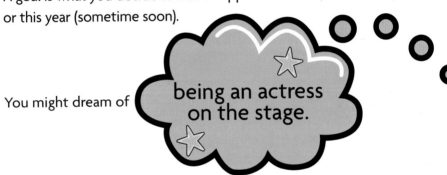 being an actress on the stage.

Think about what you can do in the near future to make that dream come true. Can you try out for a school play? Can you put on a show with friends in your neighborhood?

Look at each dream on your list. Ask, "What can I do sometime soon to work toward that dream?"

Write down your answers on pages 6 and 7 of your journal. These are your goals.

A
Can-Do
Girl

Taryn has a dream
that took her to the sea
and back.

Taryn, 11, near a manatee statue at SeaWorld

What is your dream?

I went to SeaWorld when I was six. After I saw all those *beautiful* creatures, I became really interested in sea animals. My dream is to get a job at SeaWorld.

How did you turn your dream into a goal?

I thought about ways I could learn more about sea animals. I read about them in books and on the Internet. I begged my family to go to SeaWorld again, and when we did, I met an aquarist named Tim. I've also been talking to my friend Bethany, who is a college student working toward veterinary school. It's exciting to know people who are doing the things I hope to do!

Have you set any other goals to help you reach your dream?

Yes. I'm practicing swimming, because the swim test for trainers at SeaWorld is challenging. And I would love to attend summer camp there when I'm older!

START STRONG

Go after goals BIG and small.

Small goals are things you can do today or even in the next few minutes. They're fun and build your confidence. When you say you're going to do something and you do it, you feel good about yourself. Each time you reach a small goal, you make it easier to go after the next goal.

Big goals take more time and effort. They s-t-r-e-t-c-h you and help you grow. Working toward a big goal is like reaching for something on a shelf. You can see your goal if you stand on tiptoe, but you can't reach it without effort. When you finally do, it feels REALLY good because you had to work hard and grow to get there.

Choose a good goal.

goal
goal
goal
goal
goal

A good goal is . . .

your own.

Make sure your goal is something that *you* want to do—not something you're doing to go along with your friends.

something you can do SOON.

Instead of "grow my hair long," you might decide to "find three new styles to wear my hair in while growing it out."

something to DO rather than something to STOP doing.

Instead of "stop gossiping," try "I'll be someone others trust and respect."

under your control.

If your goal is to get along well with your brother, remember that you can't control how he acts toward you. A goal you *can* control is to "be kinder to my brother."

very clear.

Make your goal clear using numbers or measurements, such as "I will say only positive things about people for seven days."

Pick a goal, and put it to the good-goal test on page 8 of your journal.

13

Write it

everywhere

and in all kinds
of ways.

The more places and ways you write your goal, the more often you'll think about it—and the more likely you'll be to make it happen.

Write it in **big, colorful letters** on index cards. Add doodles or stickers. Tape the cards everywhere—on a mirror, in your room, and in your locker.

Make yourself a **"get down to business card."** Write your goal on a small card or piece of paper, and carry it with you in your wallet or pocket.

Draw **a picture of yourself** reaching your goal. Frame the picture and put it beside your bed, or tuck the picture under your pillow for inspiration while you sleep.

15

Imagine yourself reaching your goal.

Create a mental movie in which you're the star, and imagine what it will feel like the moment that you reach your goal. Include as many details as you can.

Ask yourself these questions:

Play your movie over and over in your mind. Watch it first thing in the morning or last thing at night. Write it down, or describe it to a friend. Imagining how good it will feel to reach your goal will keep you moving forward. **Your goal will start to seem real,** and you'll KNOW that you can make it happen.

Break down your goal

into small steps

and then take ....

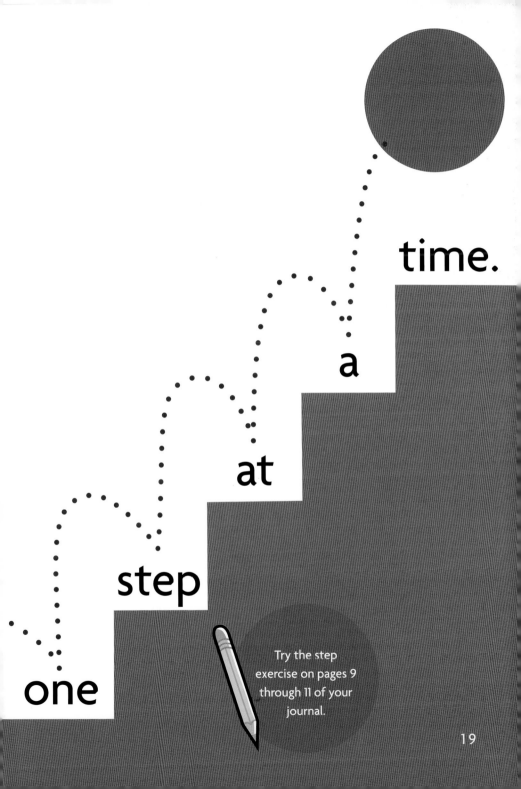

time.

a

at

step

one

Try the step
exercise on pages 9
through 11 of your
journal.

A Can-Do Girl

Meg faced her fear one step at a time.

Meg, 14, and her sister, Lila, 12, at a karaoke studio

What was your goal?

Ever since I was in preschool, I had selective mutism. That means I was too anxious to speak in certain social settings, such as school. Last fall, my mom and I started seeing an expert for help. My goal was to gain the courage to overcome my mutism.

What steps did you take to work toward your goal?

I worked toward smaller goals. First, I practiced buying things at stores. Then I called to order a pizza. Then I called different stores to see if they had something that I wanted to buy. What gave me the most courage was doing karaoke. My sister and I sang in a studio, and when we were done, our song was played on the loudspeaker in an amusement park!

When did you know you'd reached your goal?

I had so much fun doing karaoke with my sister that I thought I could do it again alone, so I did! A year ago, I would have been too nervous. I've been doing so well that when we went to see my doctor, she said we wouldn't need to see her anymore!

21

If you want to know how to make something happen, ask!

STICK WITH IT

teacher

sister

coach

friend

There are experts all around you.

neighbor

aunt

brother

grandma

Think about people who have done what you want to do. These "experts" might be in your family, your school, or your community. An expert might even be a famous person—an author or athlete or actress.

Make a list of experts, and choose two or three to speak with. Talk to your teacher after class, or chat with your sister after dinner. Don't rule out the famous people on your list. Ask a librarian to help you find an address, and write a letter asking for advice on reaching your goal. You just might get a response!

List experts on page 12 of your journal. Interview them using the questions on pages 12 and 13.

Reach out for help when you need it.

Think of three or four friends or family members who are always there for you, the ones you go to when you're feeling blue or have great news to share. These people are your "cheer squad."

Your cheer squad will . . .

help you think of fun ways to work toward your goal.

keep you focused on your goal, even when you don't feel like it.

help cheer you up if you're feeling discouraged.

remind you how far you've come.

celebrate with you when you reach your goal.

Let your cheer squad know who they are! Tell them about your goal and the steps you're taking to reach it. Ask them to help you stay on track, and check in with them through phone calls, e-mails, or visits.

Write down the names of your cheer squad on page 13 of your journal.

Be
your own
cheerleader.
Ask,

What
kinds of
things
motivate
me?

Sometimes, working toward your goal will seem easy. Other times, you'll need an extra boost of inspiration. Try these surefire motivators:

inspiration box Fill a shoebox with magazine clippings of people or things that inspire you. If your goal is to keep your room clean, cut out pictures of bedrooms that you like. Include that note from your mom thanking you for picking up your room.

token Choose a small, meaningful object to carry with you throughout the day. If you're saving money for something special, you might carry a penny. Or you might wear a ring that your friend made to remind you that she's cheering you on.

motto Make up a motto that motivates you, such as "If I dream it, I can do it." Say your motto over and over again. Make a bracelet with beads that spell out the first letter of each word in your motto. When you wear the beads, you'll FEEL the power of the words.

Face challenges

STICK WITH IT

head-on

...or find a way around them.

If you're like most people, you'll start toward your goal feeling excited and confident. But after a while, you may feel a little distracted, discouraged, or even bored.

That's NORMAL.

After all, if reaching your goal were easy, you would have done it a long time ago!

Figure out what's slowing you down by listening to that little voice in your head. What's it telling you? Read on to find out.

Watch your words.

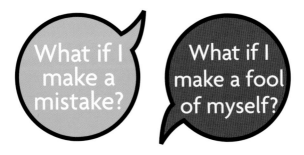

. . . **fear** is getting in your way. Put a "so" in front of your "what ifs." So what if you make a mistake? Mistakes are proof that you tried! Look at what you've learned and try again. If fear creeps in, try to push past it. Know in your heart that if you keep trying, you can reach your goal.

If you're saying . . .

. . . **procrastination** is slowing you down. Sometimes getting started is the hardest part. Do you have five minutes to practice the piano or your spelling words? Then do it! Every bit of practice adds up, makes you feel good, and keeps you moving forward.

Use **words** that give you

power.

. . . **negative words** are bringing you down. Stop them in their tracks. Replace them with words that give you power. Instead of "I can't," say "I can." Instead of "I'll never," say "I just haven't yet."

If you're saying . . .

. . . **excuses** are getting the best of you. Write them all down. Now tear them up and THROW THEM AWAY. Only YOU can stop yourself from reaching your goal. Plan for things to get in your way by saying, "If this happens, then I will do that."

Turn to pages 14 and 15 of your journal to practice making words work for you.

Don't give up!

Remember to use the many tools that you have:

 Replay your mental movie of reaching your goal. Add more details or scenes, if you like. Pretend you're starring in a sequel. What happens after you've reached your goal?

 Review your steps to see how far you've already come. Check off each step as you reach it, or use stickers to chart your progress and help you "stick to" your plan.

 Reward yourself. If your goal is to grow your nails, reward the care you've given them with a new ring or bottle of nail polish.

 Pull out your inspiration box, and look through magazines for more pieces to add to the box.

 Call someone on your cheer squad, or invite a friend over for an afternoon or a sleepover. Talk about your goals, or find a way to work toward your goal with a friend.

A Can-Do Girl

Kendal stuck with her goal—
and then set a **new** one.

Goal:
To earn
a junior
black belt
by the
age of 10

Kendal, 9, testing for her junior black belt

What was your goal?

My first goal was to become a junior black belt by age ten. I earned mine when I was nine, and then I set a new goal to get a first-degree black belt by age eleven. I earned that when I was ten!

What challenges did you face on the way to reaching your goals?

I needed to go to karate class at least three times a week, which meant I had to give up other things. And one time I had to test for a belt striping when my hand was in a cast. I had to do one-handed push-ups to qualify. I did it, though!

What has kept you motivated?

My family and friends supported me, and my instructor taught me a lot about techniques—and self-confidence. I was chosen for S.W.A.T. ("Special Winning Attitude Team"). We teach the lower-belt classes. It helps me stay motivated when I see how excited the new students get about learning a skill. Their excitement keeps me excited!

Celebrate how far you've come!

If you stick with your goal and make it happen, celebrate! Tell everyone in your cheer squad so that they can celebrate with you.

Write down how you feel the moment you reach your goal. Ask a parent to photograph you holding up your spelling test with the beautiful red A at the top, or opening that special thing you saved money for. Frame the photograph or put it in your inspiration box.

Find ways to give back. Bake cookies to share with your cheer squad, or send them thank-you notes. Offer to cheer on a friend who has goals of her own.

When you're ready, think about what's next for you. Do you want to keep working on the skills you've developed? Or do you want to choose a new goal from your list?

Be ready to rethink your

goal

. . . and start again.

You may not reach all the goals you set. Sometimes goals change. That's O.K. Remember this:

1.

Nobody reaches 100 percent of her goals—

not even a professional athlete or superstar. If you don't reach a goal, think about what you've learned. Did you do things you thought you couldn't? Did you have fun? What will you do differently next time?

2.

Not reaching a goal is different from failing.

The only way to truly fail is to not try at all. So get up and get moving again. Find a goal that's a better fit for you, and go after it!

Try another way of going after a goal:

together.

Working toward goals with friends is not that different from working toward goals on your own.

Team goal-setting is like a relay race. Each of you has your own goal, your own part of the race to run. If each of you runs as fast as you can and meets your goal, then the whole team meets its goal.

Remember: The more people you have working toward a goal, the more fun you'll have, and the BIGGER the goal that you can accomplish.

Turn to page 16 in your journal to set some team goals with friends.

Can-Do Girls

Ashley, Krista, and Britta got down to business—together!

Chickadee Spa

From left: Britta, Krista, and Ashley, all 13, of Chickadee Spa

What was your group goal?

We started a business together called Chickadee Spa. We specialize in face painting, painting nails, and doing hair at birthday parties for younger girls. The business has been a big success, and we hope to keep it growing. Our next steps are to do more advertising and purchase some new supplies.

Does each of you have a certain job to do?

Krista keeps all of the supplies, while Ashley is in charge of the paperwork. We also have our specialties when doing hair and nails. Krista specializes in doing messy buns, and Britta does French braids. When we do nails, Ashley paints dice, Britta paints stripes, and Krista paints stars.

How is going after goals more fun with friends?

We keep each other excited by talking about the business and making future plans. And when the business is going really well, we celebrate together. We spent part of our first paycheck at Darla's, a local malt shop!

If you didn't know it before,
you know it now—you can do just about
ANYTHING, as long as you choose smart goals,
take them one step at a time, and remember
to ask for help when you need it.

Keep stretching, learning, and growing. Set goals,
reach them, and then set NEW goals.
Believe that you can, and help other girls
believe that they can, too.

Each goal you reach will bring you
one step closer to making your
dreams come TRUE.

Write to us!

Tell us about the goals you've set and how you made them happen. What motivated you? Who helped you along the way?

Send letters to:
You Can Do It! Editor
American Girl
8400 Fairway Place
Middleton, WI 53562

Here are some other American Girl books you might like:

❏ I read it.

❏ I read it.

❏ I read it.

❏ I read it.

❏ I read it.

❏ I read it.

❏ I read it.

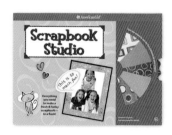

❏ I read it.